The Storm

by Sally Vargas
illustrated by Sue Williams

The sky was dark.
Rick said, "Looks like rain!"

"It is going to storm,"
Bella said.

Mom said, "Let's bring everything inside. Then it will stay safe."

Bella helped Mom carry the table.

Rick said, "I'll put away
Kelly's bike."
He put his bat and ball
away, too.

Rick looked around.
Everything was put away.
It would all be safe.

"What if the lights go out?"
Rick asked.

"I hope they do. We will
see with flashlights!"
Bella said.

The night was black.
The wind bent the trees.
Rain hit the house hard.

Mom read books aloud.
Dad made sandwiches.

Rick said, "We are fine!
But I hope the sun comes
back tomorrow!"